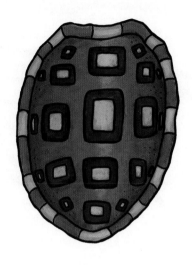

You look at me and see just a shell.
But, I warn you, my friend,
you don't know me so well!
                    -Juani the Tortoise

www.rourkepublishing.com

Editor: Frank Sloan

The Monkey's New Drum is based on a tale from Panama included in *El Folklore Panameño en Función de las Teorias Freudianas* by Luisa Aguilera de Santos, 1963

To Nicky Stratford, with gratitude
   -S.S.

Library of Congress Cataloging-in-Publication Data

Sepehri, Sandy.
   The monkey's new drum : based on a trickster tale from Panama / retold by
Sandy Sepehri ; illustrated by Brian Demeter.
      p. cm. -- (Latin American tales and myths)
   ISBN 1-60044-214-5
   1. Tales--Panama. 2. Tricksters--Panama. I. Demeter, Brian, ill. II.
Title. III. Series.

   GR118.P2S47 2007
   398.2097287--dc22

                              2006014659

Printed in the USA

PO 76118   11/06/06

Latin American Tales
and Myths

The Monkey's New Drum

Based On A Trickster Tale From Panama

Retold by Sandy Sepehri
Illustrated by Brian Demeter
Cover design and storyboards
by Nicola Stratford
Project Consultant:
Silvina Peralta Ramos

Rourke
Publishing LLC
Vero Beach, Florida 32964

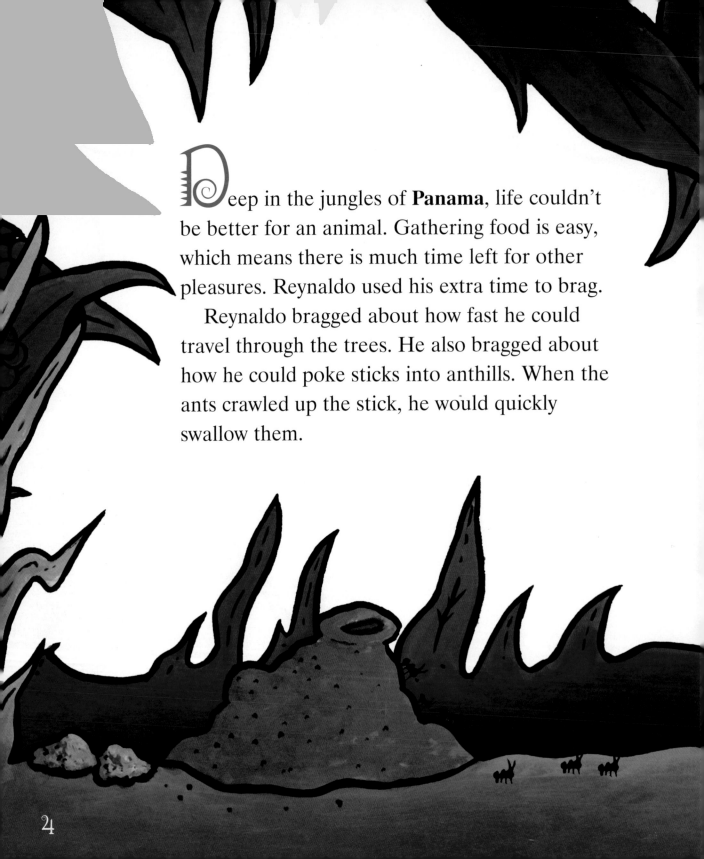

Deep in the jungles of **Panama**, life couldn't be better for an animal. Gathering food is easy, which means there is much time left for other pleasures. Reynaldo used his extra time to brag.

Reynaldo bragged about how fast he could travel through the trees. He also bragged about how he could poke sticks into anthills. When the ants crawled up the stick, he would quickly swallow them.

Reynaldo thought he was the most intelligent animal in all of Panama! He would spend countless hours combing his fingers through his hair, picking through it for bugs. When he looked at the reflection of his face in the water he was very pleased with himself. "There's not a finer looking animal in all Panama," he would croon.

There was only one thing Reynaldo loved to do more than compliment himself. That was to insult animals that were smaller and slower than he was, like **Juani** the tortoise. Whenever Juani crawled slowly by, Reynaldo would jeer at him.

Juani, Juani, the moving stone,
His dirty shell is his only home.

Juani, Juani, I have heard it said
There's nothing but chewed-up grass inside your head!

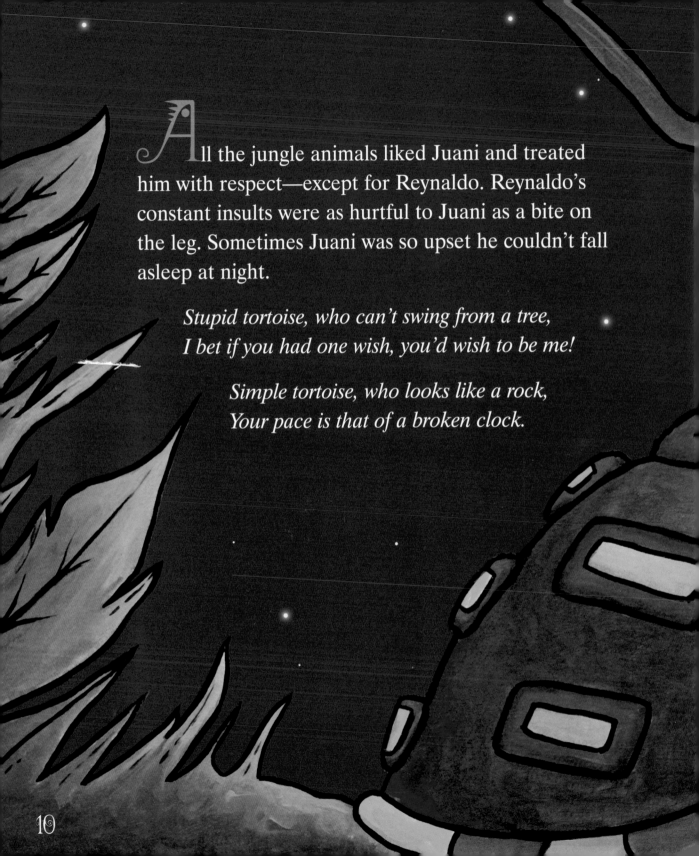

All the jungle animals liked Juani and treated him with respect—except for Reynaldo. Reynaldo's constant insults were as hurtful to Juani as a bite on the leg. Sometimes Juani was so upset he couldn't fall asleep at night.

Stupid tortoise, who can't swing from a tree,
I bet if you had one wish, you'd wish to be me!

Simple tortoise, who looks like a rock,
Your pace is that of a broken clock.

One morning Juani was so sad he decided not to come out of his shell. But his plan was foiled by **Cuaco**, the hermit crab, who came to visit.

When Juani heard Cuaco's voice, Juani poked his head out of his shell.

"**Lo siento**, Cuaco," said Juani. "Please don't think I'm rude. I just want to be left alone."

"Why do you hide from the world when it is so beautiful?" asked Cuaco.

"Because Reynaldo calls me slow," explained Juani.

"Impossible," shouted Cuaco. "You are one of my fastest friends! Why, it takes me a whole day to travel the ground you cover in just one hour."

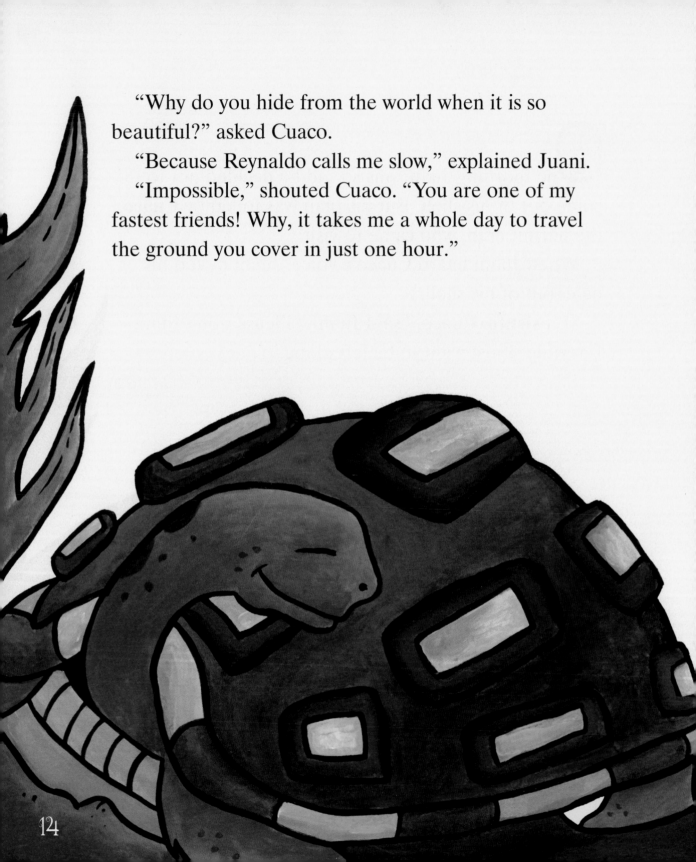

"He calls me stupid," Juani complained.

"Why does he say you are stupid?" demanded Cuaco.

"He also says I am ugly and look like a rock."

"But you are the jewel of the jungle. Your shell has a beautiful pattern. And it protects you like a suit of armor.

"What Reynaldo says about you is not true!" Cuaco said. "It is time to teach this monkey a lesson."

"But how?" asked Juani.

"Challenge him to a wager you know you can win," answered Cuaco. "Choose something that a tortoise can do better than a monkey."

"What should I wager with?" asked Juani.

"The shell of your **abuelo**!" answered Cuaco.

"But why should he want my grandfather's shell?"

"To Reynaldo it is a treasure," answered Cuaco. "I have seen him try to steal it many times, but always a puma walks by or an alligator rises up from his nap and scares him away."

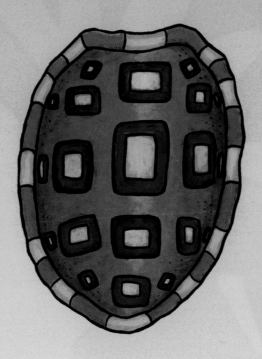

"What would he want with it?" Juani demanded.

"I have heard him say he could use it as a drum. So, make a wager with Reynaldo, but don't let him win! You will keep the shell, and Reynaldo will learn to show some respect."

Juani felt much better after Cuaco's pep talk. But what could he do better than a monkey? This would take much planning.

But there was no time, because Juani suddenly saw Reynaldo hanging from a **mango** tree. Reynaldo spoke:

Juani, Juani - last is the place
That you would take against me in a race.

"A race?" thought Juani to himself. "**Sì**, a race he cannot win!" This time, instead of crawling away with his feelings and his head hanging down, Juani looked up at Reynaldo and replied:

You look at me and see just a shell.
But, I warn you, my friend, you don't know me so well!

I may be different from you,
But my worth is no less.
If you do not believe it,
Let us put it to a test!

"A test, you say?" shouted Reynaldo as he jumped down from the mango tree.

"We shall race up the mango tree," shouted Juani. "If I win, you must stop insulting me. If you win, you may have my grandfather's tortoise shell!"

"**¡Caramba! Vámonos**, then. Let's go!" Reynaldo shouted.

Reynaldo climbed up the tree as naturally as the tide rolls upon the shore. He was sitting on the winner's branch for a long, long time, waiting for Juani. While he waited, he pictured himself drumming upon his new tortoise shell, making fine party music.

"Surely everyone will come to my **fiestas** once they hear the music from my new drum," thought Reynaldo to himself.

Finally, after much huffing and puffing,
Juani pulled himself up next to Reynaldo.
"If you are not too tired, Reynaldo, will
you make one more bet with me?"
Juani asked.

"What now?" asked Reynaldo.

24

"Will you bet me the return of my grandfather's shell if I beat you in a race back to the ground?"

"Why not? I have to climb back down the tree anyway."

"**G**racias, Reynaldo. On the count of three: **Uno, dos, tres**, vámanos!" said Juani.

As Reynaldo began climbing down the tree, Juani flung himself from the branch. He quickly pulled his head and feet into his shell and hit the ground with the speed of a lightning bolt.

Landing unharmed, Juani realized that his shell was indeed a treasure. He pushed his face out and watched Reynaldo reach the ground.

Without boasting, Juani simply began his slow walk home. He was pleased with his trick, but he felt sad to see Reynaldo so miserable and alone.

The very next night Reynaldo was throwing a party – all by himself. Juani found him sitting against his mango tree, with plenty of mangoes to eat and **papaya** juice to drink. All that was missing was a group of friends to share it with. Juani approached him, with a large object wrapped in **plantain** leaves.

"I have a gift for you, Reynaldo," said Juani, with a smile.

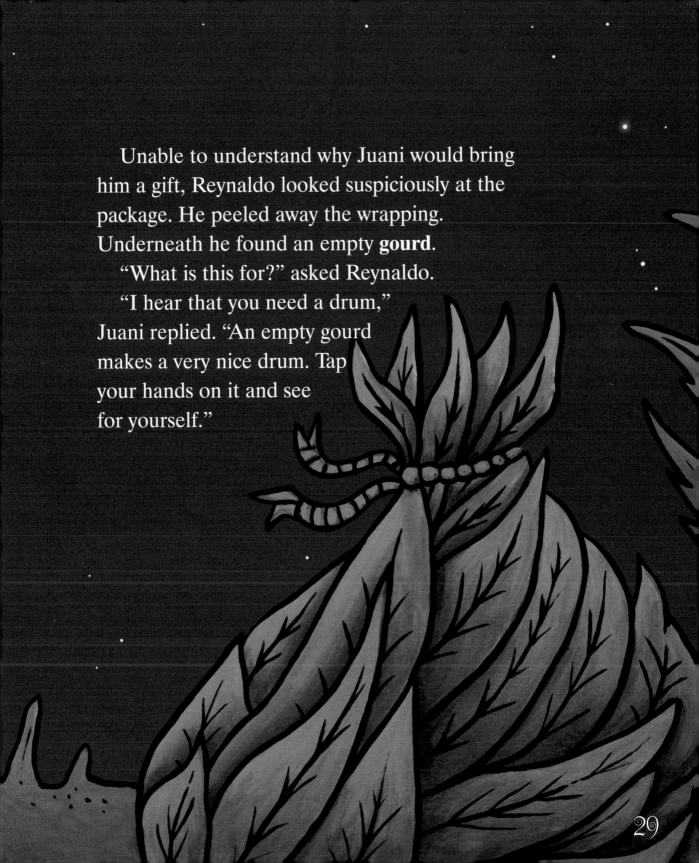

Unable to understand why Juani would bring him a gift, Reynaldo looked suspiciously at the package. He peeled away the wrapping. Underneath he found an empty **gourd**.

"What is this for?" asked Reynaldo.

"I hear that you need a drum," Juani replied. "An empty gourd makes a very nice drum. Tap your hands on it and see for yourself."

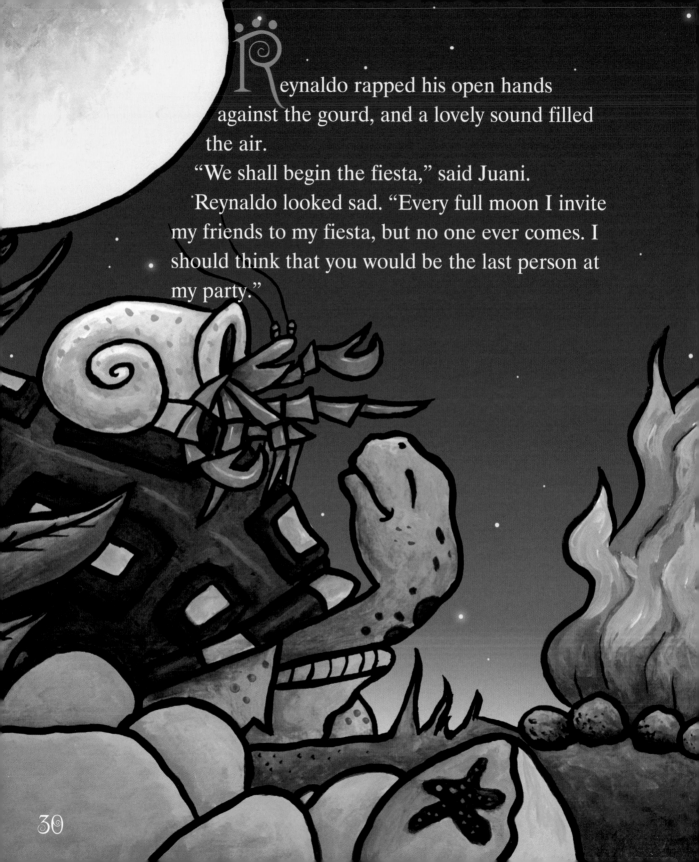

Reynaldo rapped his open hands against the gourd, and a lovely sound filled the air.

"We shall begin the fiesta," said Juani.

Reynaldo looked sad. "Every full moon I invite my friends to my fiesta, but no one ever comes. I should think that you would be the last person at my party."

"I will be the first," corrected Juani. "And, as you learn how one friend should treat another, your fiestas will become too big for all of Panama!"

Then the tortoise and the monkey helped themselves to the sweet mangoes and papaya juice while they listened to the joyful rhythm of Reynaldo's new drum.

Glossary

abuelo (ab WAY loe) – grandfather

¡caramba! (car AHM bah) – I say!

cuaco (koo AH koe) – hermit crab

fiestas (fee EH stahz) – parties

gourd (gord) – fruit, often dried and hollowed for use
 as a drinking cup

gracias (GRAHS see ahs) – thank you

Juani (WAH nee) – Johnny

lo siento (loe see EN toe) – I'm sorry

mango (mang GO) – sweet tropical fruit with a large
 center seed

Panama (PAN a ma) – a nation in Central America,
 bordering both the Caribbean Sea and the North Pacific
 Ocean, between Colombia and Costa Rica.

papaya (pah PIE yah) – large fruit originating with the
 Native Americans.

plantain (plan TAYNE) – a banana-like tropical fruit

sí (see) – yes

Uno, dos, tres (ooh NO, DOSE, TRACE) – one, two, three

vámonos (vahm AHN noes) – let's go

About The Author

Sandy Sepehri lives with her husband, Shahram, and their
three children in Florida. She has a bachelor's degree and
writes freelance articles and children's stories.